Can an aardvark BARK?

Melissa Stewart

illustrated by Steve Jenkins

Beach Lane Books

New York London Toronto Sydney New Delhi

Can an aardvark **bark?**

An **aardvark** grunts softly as it zigzags across African grasslands at night. When it sniffs out an ant nest or termite mound, it laps up thousands of insects with its long, sticky tongue.

No, but it can grunt.

Lots of other animals grunt too.

Grunts. Growls. Chuckles. Chirps. A **river otter** makes all these sounds—and more. It usually grunts while it's playing or grooming.

Hamadryas baboons travel and sleep in large groups called bands. When two members of the same band meet, they greet one another with a series of low, soft grunts.

A **white-tailed deer** grunts for all kinds of reasons. A low grunt means, "I'm the boss! Do what I say." A friendlier grunt means, "I'm over here. Where are you?"

An **oyster toadfish** spends most of its time waiting quietly for prey to pass by. But when the fish feels angry or afraid, it makes a low grunting sound that blows its cover.

Can a seal squeal?

No, but it can **bark.**

At mating time, a male **New Zealand fur seal** works hard to defend his spot on the beach. If another male gets too close, the seal rises up on his front flippers and barks at the intruder.

Lots of other animals **bark** too.

When a **capybara** senses danger, it belts out a series of rasping barks. The warning tells the rest of its herd, "Head for the water and swim to safety!"

Common barking geckos rest underground all day long. As the sun sets, a male comes out of his burrow and barks to let other geckos know where he is.

During spring rains, a male **barking tree frog** attracts a female with loud calls that sound like a small dog. Then the couple mates in a nearby wetland.

When **woodchucks** feel scared, they belt out a high-pitched whistle. But they often bark and squeal while fighting with one another.

Can a wild boar **roar?**

No, but it can **squeal**.

When a **wild boar** feels safe and calm, it grunts softly. But when it feels excited or scared, it squeals loudly.

Lots of other animals **squeal** too.

A **European hedgehog** snorts when it's angry and purrs when it's happy. When the prickly critter senses danger, it squeals and rolls up in a tight ball.

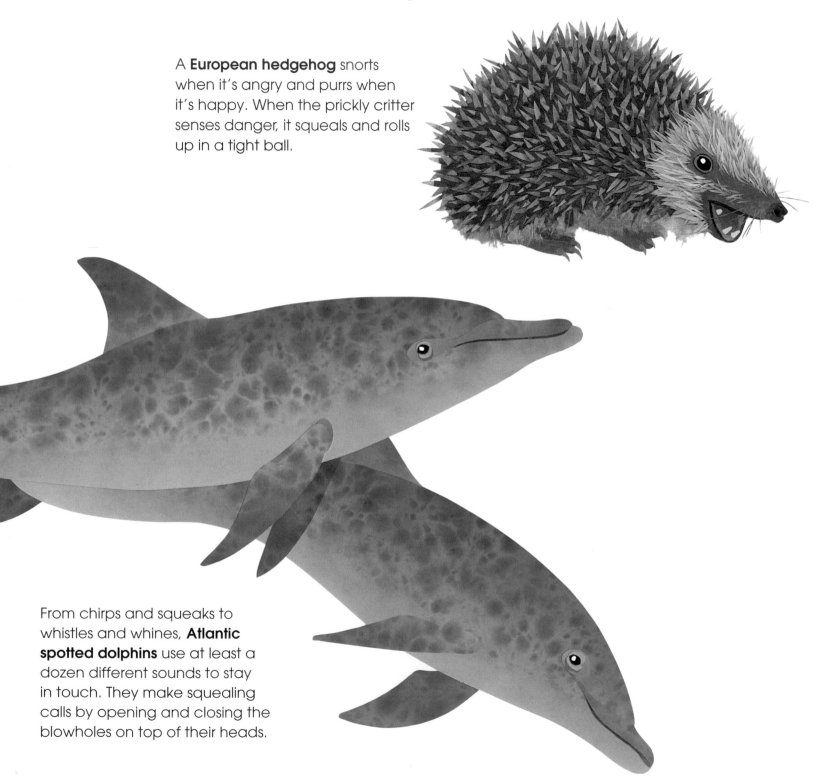

From chirps and squeaks to whistles and whines, **Atlantic spotted dolphins** use at least a dozen different sounds to stay in touch. They make squealing calls by opening and closing the blowholes on top of their heads.

After a male and female **Abert's towhee** spend time apart, they greet each other with a series of squeals that say, "I missed you. I'm so happy you're home."

A **margay** has a trick for catching its dinner. It makes a high-pitched squeal pretending to be a baby pied tamarin monkey. When the adult monkeys come to investigate, the hungry hunter attacks.

Can a porcupine **whine**?

Why, yes, it **can!**

Each autumn, **African crested porcupine** males fight for the right to mate with a female. The winner whines and stomps his tail. If the female seems interested, he sprays her with urine, and she lowers her quills so he can get close.

Lots of other animals whine too.

Black bear cubs scream when they're upset and hum when they're happy. Some cubs get whiny when they see their mom. Others whine while wrestling with their brothers and sisters.

When a baby **beaver** needs food, it whines to its mama, and the message is clear: "I'm hungry. Can I have a snack?"

How does a **mosquito** make its annoying whine? By beating its wings. The pesky insects probably use the noise to find one another.

When two **American martens** meet, they huff, chuckle, pant, and growl at one another. If the smaller, weaker animal is smart, it whines and backs away.

Can a dingo bellow?

A **dingo** barks less than a pet dog, but it often howls, growls, whimpers, and whines. When a male dingo growls, he's usually reminding his family that he's in charge.

No, but it can **growl.**

Lots of other animals **growl** too.

Some snakes hiss. Others shake their rattle. But when the eighteen-foot-long **king cobra** is about to strike, it makes a low, growling moan.

A **platypus** spends its nights swimming through rivers in search of earthworms, shrimp, and crayfish. The strange-looking mammal growls softly when something surprises or disturbs it.

An **ostrich** usually keeps quiet. But at mating time, a male growls like a lion when other males set foot in his territory.

A **coastal giant salamander** may look like a peaceful creature, but it knows how to put up a fight. The angry amphibian arches its back, growls at its rival, and lashes out with its poisonous tail.

Can a giraffe **laugh**?

No, but it can **bellow**.

Giraffes are usually quiet animals. But if a youngster gets lost, it makes a long, sad, bleating call. And its mom quickly answers with a loud, roaring bellow.

Lots of other animals **bellow** too.

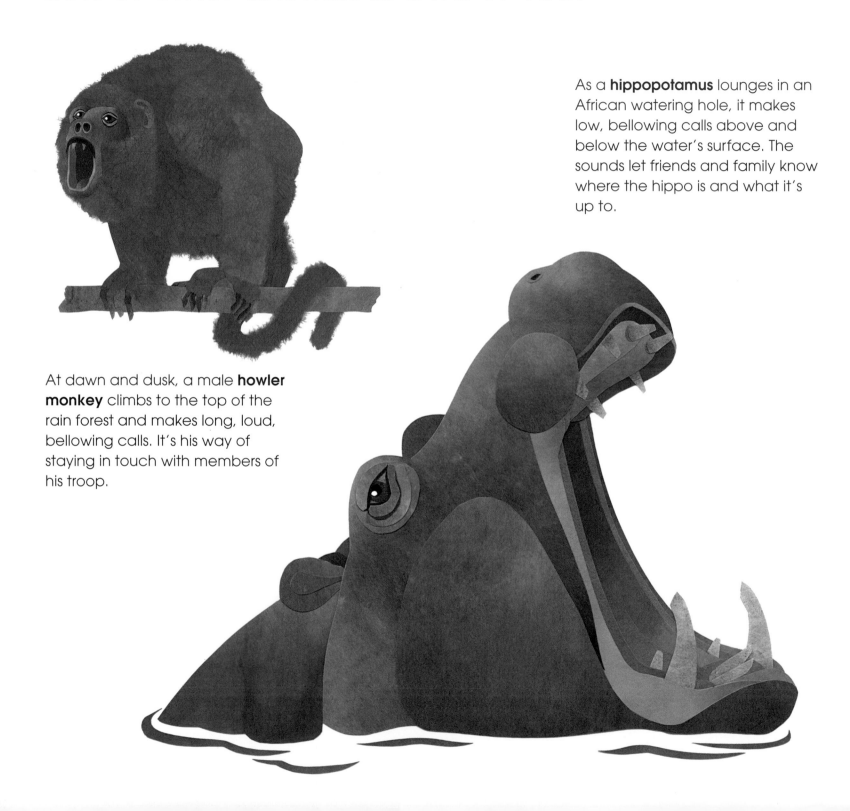

As a **hippopotamus** lounges in an African watering hole, it makes low, bellowing calls above and below the water's surface. The sounds let friends and family know where the hippo is and what it's up to.

At dawn and dusk, a male **howler monkey** climbs to the top of the rain forest and makes long, loud, bellowing calls. It's his way of staying in touch with members of his troop.

A male **koala** really makes a racket at mating time. His deep, growling bellow helps females find him.

When a female **moose** is looking for a mate, she belts out loud, moaning bellows that say, "I'm over here! Come find me!"

Can a kangaroo **mew**?

No, but it can laugh.

An **eastern gray kangaroo** may grunt, cough, or hiss depending on its mood. But when a joey spots its mom, it lets out an excited laughing sound.

Lots of other animals laugh too...

At dawn and dusk, a **laughing kookaburra** calls out with a series of low chuckles and loud laughs. It's the bird's way of saying, "Here I am. This is my home."

After catching prey, a **spotted hyena** celebrates by making a high-pitched laughing call. The sound invites other hyenas to come join the feast.

When **rats** play with one another, they make high-pitched chirping chortles to express their glee.

What happens when a papa **gorilla** tickles his baby? The little one squirms, swats playfully at his hand, and makes soft, rumbling giggles.

can you?

laugh

grunt

bellow

growl

squeal

bark

whine

Animals use all kinds of sounds to communicate their thoughts and feelings. Just like you!